# GREAT ILLUSTRATED CLASSICS

# TREASURE ISLAND

## Robert Louis Stevenson

adapted by
**Deidre S. Laiken**

Illustrations by
A. J. McAllister

BARONET BOOKS, New York, New York

# GREAT ILLUSTRATED CLASSICS

**edited by
Malvina G. Vogel**

# CONTENTS

## About the Author

Robert Louis Stevenson was born in Edinburgh, Scotland, on November 13, 1850. Since he was a frail young man, he could not follow the family profession of engineering. Instead he became a writer and a traveler.

Stevenson married an American woman and wrote *Treasure Island* for his stepson. The book made Stevenson famous, but he also became well known for his essays, poems and short stories. He died at the age of forty-four on the island of Samoa.

Robert Louis Stevenson wrote other classic novels that are known and loved by children and grownups all over the world. They include *Kidnapped*, *The Black Arrow*, and *Dr. Jekyll and Mr. Hyde*.

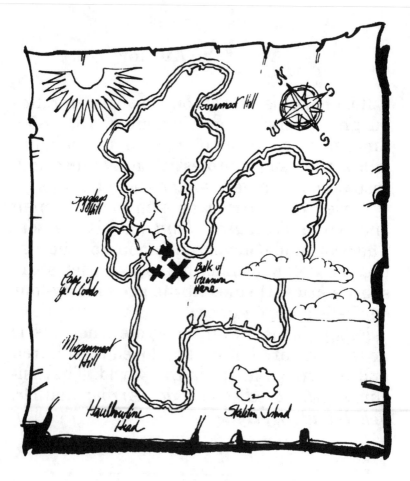

Treasure Island

## Characters You Will Meet

Jim Hawkins, *the boy who tells the story*
Jim's Mother
Billy Bones, *a pirate called the Captain*

Dr. Livesey
Squire Trelawney     *Jim's friends who go with him to Treasure Island*

Black Dog, *a strange visitor*
Pew, *the blind man*
Long John Silver, *the one-legged pirate*
Captain Smollett, *the captain of the* Hispaniola
Ben Gunn, *the man of Treasure Island*
*Sailors on the* Hispaniola
    Arrow
    Israel Hands
    Redruth
    Hunter
    Joyce
    Gray

A Story Begins.

# Chapter 1
## A Visitor to the Inn

I am writing this story about Treasure Island on the request of my friends, Squire Trelawney and Dr. Livesey. All of the things I shall tell happened to me many years ago.

It all began when I, Jim Hawkins, was just a boy and my father ran the Admiral Benbow Inn. I remember it as if it were yesterday. A large, heavy man burst in the inn door. He carried a large sea chest and wore a soiled blue coat. His hands were ragged and scarred, and his fingernails were black and broken. He had a white scar across one cheek. I remember him looking around and whistling to himself. Then he broke out in that old sea-song that he sang so often:

"Fifteen men on the Dead Man's Chest,
Yo-ho-ho, and a bottle of rum!"

After finishing his song, he asked for a bottle of rum and introduced himself. He told us only that we should call him "captain." He threw several gold coins on the table, and my father showed him to his room.

The captain stayed with us for a long time. He was a silent man by custom. All day long he hung around the cove or sat on the cliffs with a brass telescope. During the evening, he sat by the fire and drank rum and water. Every day when he came back from his stroll he would ask if any seafaring men had passed by. I soon figured out that the captain asked this question because he was hiding from someone or something.

One day he took me aside and promised me

Captain

a silver coin on the first of every month if I would only keep my eye out for a seafaring man with one leg and let him know the moment he appeared.

The image of this frightening person haunted my dreams and caused me many sleepless nights. On stormy nights, when the wind shook the four corners of the house and the surf roared along the cove and up the cliffs, I would see the one-legged man in a thousand forms. Sometimes the leg would be cut off at the knee, other times at the hip, and still other times I imagined him as a monstrous creature who had only one leg which grew from the middle of his body.

But although I was terrified by the idea of the seafaring man with one leg, I was far less afraid of the captain than were most people who came to the inn. His stories frightened them. They were dreadful tales about hanging, walking the plank, and wild storms at

Terrifying Dreams

sea. When the captain told his tales, he grew red in the face, and his voice boomed like cannon fire. Although the people were frightened at the time, when I look back I realize that the stories provided their dull country lives with some excitement and adventure.

The captain stayed with us many months. After a while he had no more gold coins, but my poor father was too afraid to ask him to leave. All the time he stayed with us, the captain never changed his clothes, except for his socks. His coat was patched and re-patched, but never replaced. He never wrote or received a letter, and he spoke only with patrons of the inn.

During these months, Dr. Livesey visited us many times. My father was very sick, and we all feared he would never live to see the spring. The doctor took an immediate dislike to the captain. One evening the two men got into a quarrel. In a fit of temper the captain

Telling Exciting Tales

drew a sharp sailor's knife from his pocket and threatened to pin the doctor to the wall.

The doctor never so much as moved. He spoke in his usual calm tone of voice:

"If you do not put that knife away, I promise, upon my honor, that you shall hang for your actions."

The two men stared silently at each other, but the captain soon knuckled under, put away his knife, and sat down. All the while he grumbled like a beaten dog.

The Captain's Threat

A Bitter Cold Winter

## Chapter 2
## Black Dog

It was not long after this that there occurred the first of the mysterious events that rid us at last of the captain. It was a bitter cold winter. Hard frosts came and heavy gales blew around the little cove. I knew that my poor father had not long to live.

One cold January morning, a pale, thin man came to the inn door. He was missing two fingers from his left hand, and he spoke in a quiet but determined manner. He asked me first what my name was. When I replied "Jim Hawkins," he nodded as if he already knew this. Then he asked me to bring him a glass of rum. After he drained the glass he looked up at me and said:

"Come here, Jim. Is this table over here for my mate Bill?"

I told him I did not know his mate Bill. The only person who lived at the inn besides my family was the captain. I then described the captain. The man smiled in recognition.

"That's my mate Bill, all right," he said. "You and I will just go back into the parlor, Jim, and we'll get behind the door and give Bill a little surprise when he comes in."

So the stranger and I hid behind the large oak parlor door.

At last, in strode the captain, slamming the door behind him. He looked straight ahead as he headed right for the breakfast table.

"Bill!" said the stranger in a loud voice.

The captain spun around on his heel and

Hiding Behind the Parlor Door

faced us. He turned totally white. He had the look of a man who had just seen a ghost.

"Come, Bill, you know me. You must remember your old shipmate," said the stranger.

The captain gasped.

"Black Dog!" he said.

"That's right," laughed the stranger. "And I think it's time we had a little talk."

With that, Black Dog asked me to bring two glasses of rum so he and the captain could have their little talk. When I returned with the rum, they were already seated on either side of the table.

For a long time, though I certainly did my best to listen, I could hear nothing but low voices. Soon the voices grew louder and louder.

Then all of a sudden there was a tremendous explosion of curses and other noises. The chair and the table went over in a crash. A clash of steel followed and then a cry of pain,

Black Dog!

and the next instant I saw Black Dog in full flight. The captain was running after him, and both men had drawn swords. Blood was streaming from Black Dog's left shoulder. As they reached the door, the captain aimed a blow at Black Dog that surely would have cut him in two, had it not been for the low-hanging signboard of the Admiral Benbow Inn. You can see the notch on the lower side of the frame to this day.

Once out on the road, Black Dog, in spite of his wound, ran away and disappeared over the edge of the hill. The captain stood staring at the signboard like a bewildered man.

He passed his hand over his eyes and shouted for me to bring him some rum and to be quick about it. The next thing I heard was a loud fall in the parlor. I ran in and saw the captain lying full length upon the floor. At that instant, my mother came running downstairs to help me. Between us we raised

The Captain Was Lying on the Floor.

the captain's head. He was breathing very loudly, but his eyes were closed and his face was drained of all color.

"Dear, dear!" cried my mother. "What a disgrace upon the house! And with your poor father so sick."

It was a great relief to us when the door opened and Dr. Livesey came in to pay a visit to my father.

"Oh, doctor," I cried, "what shall we do? Where is he wounded?"

The doctor soon discovered that the captain had not been wounded at all. He had had a stroke. In no time at all, the doctor rolled up the captain's sleeve and prepared to take some blood. On the captain's arm we noticed many tattoos. One said, "Here's luck," another, "A fair wind," and a third said, "Billy Bones, his fancy."

From that tattoo we figured out that Billy Bones must be the captain's real name. In a

Dr. Livesey Came In to Pay a Visit.

little while the captain came to, and we managed to hoist him upstairs and put him in his bed. The doctor warned all of us that any rum drinking would be the death of the captain. He also confided in me that the old sailor would have to stay in bed for at least a week, or he might suffer still another stroke.

Dr. Livesey's Warning

The Captain Asks for Rum.

## Chapter 3
## The Black Spot

The next afternoon I stopped to bring the captain some cooling drinks and medicine. He was lying very much as we had left him the day before. Although he was still weak, he seemed excited.

"Jim," he said, "you're the only one here that I can depend upon. You know that I have given you a silver coin every month I've been here. I'm pretty low now, but do you think you could bring me a glass of rum?"

I tried to tell him what the doctor had said, but he dismissed it as nonsense. As he talked and tried to convince me how badly he needed the rum, his voice grew louder. I was thinking only of my father, who needed quiet, and I agreed to get him the rum if he would be still. Then he asked me how long the doctor said he would be in bed. When I told him it would be at least a week, he looked angry.

"Thunder!" he cried. "A week's more than I have. They will have the black spot on me by then. I won't let 'em get me this time, I swear to it!"

As he was speaking, he tried to get out of bed, but he collapsed in weakness.

"Jim," he said, "that Black Dog, he was a bad one, but there are worse out there to get me. Now, if I can't get away, they'll tip me the black spot. Mind you, it's my old sea chest that they're after. You get on a horse and go to that doctor. Tell him to send all the men he can find here to the inn. All of old Flint's crew will be here. I was Flint's first mate,

Collapsing from Weakness

and I'm the only one who knows where it is. He gave it to me as he died. But don't tell this to anyone unless they give me the black spot or you see Black Dog or that man with the one leg."

None of this made any sense to me at all. I asked him again and again what the black spot was and who Flint was, but he slowly drifted into sleep.

I scarcely had time to think about what the captain had told me, when my poor father in the other room took a turn for the worse and died suddenly.

My sadness, the visits of our friends, and all the details of the funeral made me forget my strange conversation with the captain.

So things passed until the day after the funeral. At about three o'clock, I was standing at the door, full of sad thoughts about my father, when I saw someone coming towards the inn. He was obviously blind, for he tapped

Full of Sad Thoughts

in front of himself with a stick and wore dark glasses over his eyes. He was hunched over and wore a huge tattered seacloak with a hood. I never saw a more dreadful-looking creature. He stopped a little ways from the inn and said in a singsong voice:

"Will someone tell a poor blind man where or in what part of this country he is?"

I told the man that he was at the Admiral Benbow Inn in Black Hill Cove. With that, he asked me to show him inside. When he gripped my hand, he held on like a vise and pulled me close to him.

"Now, boy," he said, "take me to the captain."

I tried to refuse, but he gave me a wrench that made me cry out. Then, holding me with his iron grasp, he made me lead him upstairs to the sick man's room.

When the captain raised his eyes, I saw in them a look of fear and weakness. He tried to rise, but did not have the strength.

A Dreadful-Looking Creature!

"Now, Bill, sit where you are," said the blind man. "Even though I can't see, I can hear if you move a finger. Now you, Jim, take his left hand and bring it close to mine."

We both obeyed him to the letter, and I saw him pass something from his hand to the captain's hand.

"And now that's done," said the blind man. And he walked slowly out of the inn. I could hear his stick tap-tap-tapping into the distance.

It was some time before either I or the captain seemed to gather our senses. When I let go of his wrist, he drew in his hand and looked into the palm.

"Ten o'clock!" he cried. "Six hours. I'll escape them yet!" And he sprang to his feet.

As he did this, he grabbed at his throat, swayed for a moment, and then fell with a loud thud upon the floor.

I ran to him at once and called my mother.

Passing Something from Hand to Hand

The captain had died of a stroke! Although I never liked the man, when I saw him there on the floor I burst into a flood of tears. It was the second death I had known, and the sorrow of the first was still fresh in my heart.

A Second Death

Too Frightened to Stay in the House!

## Chapter 4
## The Sea Chest

I lost no time, of course, in telling my mother all that I knew about the captain and his strange visitors. Some of the dead man's money—if he had any—was certainly due us. I could not ride away to the doctor's, as the captain had asked me to do, since it would leave my mother unprotected and alone. Both of us were too frightened to stay in the house. The dead body on the parlor floor and the thought of that blind man hovering near and ready to return filled us with all sorts of fears. So the two of us ran out into the frosty evening to get help from some of the villagers.

When we reached the village, I felt relieved to see the yellow lights in doors and windows. But to our disappointment, no one would return with us to the inn. After I told my story, everyone turned away in fear. The name of Captain Flint was well known to some of the people there. Several of the men had heard tales of cruelty about him and his infamous crew.

After everyone declined to return with us, my mother stood up and with great courage declared that she would not lose the money that rightfully belonged to her fatherless son.

"If none of the rest of you dare," she said, "Jim and I will go back. Small thanks to you big, hulking, chicken-hearted men. We'll open that chest, if we have to die doing it."

Of course I went with my mother, but my heart was thumping with fear as we set out in the cold night. We slipped along the hedges

No Help from the Villagers

silently and swiftly. But we did not see or hear anything to increase our terrors, and soon we were safely back inside the inn.

I slipped the bolt at once, and we stood and panted for a moment in the dark. We were alone with the dead captain's body. Then my mother lit a candle, and holding each other's hands, we advanced into the parlor. He lay as we had left him—on his back, with his eyes open and one arm stretched out.

"Draw the blinds, Jim," whispered my mother. "We have to get the key off his body. It must be there somewhere."

I went down on my knees at once. On the floor close to his hand there was a little piece of paper. It was blackened on one side. This must have been the black spot. On the other side was written this short message:

YOU HAVE TILL TEN TONIGHT.

I looked up at the clock. It was almost six. We still had four hours.

Alone with the Dead Body

I felt in the dead man's pockets, but all I found were some coins and bits of tobacco.

"Perhaps it's around his neck," suggested my mother.

I closed my eyes as I tore open his shirt. Sure enough, hanging on a bit of string was a small silver key. I cut the string and we hurried upstairs to open the chest.

It was like any other seaman's chest on the outside. The initial "B" was burned on the top with a hot iron, and the corners were smashed and broken. We unlocked the lid and opened the chest.

A strong smell of tobacco rose from inside. We unpacked the contents layer by layer. There were some clothes, pistols, a Spanish watch, a compass and many trinkets. But at the very bottom we found a bundle of papers tied up in an oilcloth sack and a purse filled with gold coins.

"I'll show these rascals that I'm an honest

Opening the Chest

woman," said my mother. "I'll only take what he owed us and not a penny more."

She began to count out the amount from the captain's debt. It was a difficult task, since the coins came from so many different countries, and neither of us knew their exact worth. When we were about halfway through, I suddenly heard a sound. It was the tap-tapping of the blind man's stick upon the frozen road. I urged my mother to take the money and make a fast escape. But my mother, frightened as she was, was unwilling to take a cent more or a cent less than was rightfully due us. But when she heard the sound of approaching footsteps, she decided to take what she had already counted. I kept the papers in the oilcloth sack, and we left by the back door.

We had only reached the outside of the inn when we could hear a group of men knocking at the front door. My mother and I began to run.

Escaping with the Oilcloth Sack

"My dear," she said, "take the money and the papers and run on ahead. I am going to faint." But I wouldn't leave her.

This was certainly the end for both of us, I thought. Somehow, we made it to the little wooden bridge and I helped her across. As soon as we reached the other side, she collapsed in a dead faint. I managed to drag her to a spot where we could not be seen, but where we could hear everything that was going on inside the inn.

Jim Helps His Mother Across the Bridge.

Men Were Pounding at the Inn Door.

## Chapter 5
## The Last of the Blind Man

My curiosity was greater than my fear, and I crept even closer to the inn, so that I could see and hear what was happening.

There were seven or eight men pounding at the heavy oak door. Even through the mist, I could see the blind man. I heard his voice as he shouted to break down the door. The men obeyed him, and in a flash the door was ripped from its hinges.

Once they were inside, I heard one of the men shout in surprise that Bill was dead.

"Search him and find the chest!" cried the blind man.

A few seconds later, the window of the captain's room was thrown open, and a man leaned out and shouted that someone had already gotten to the chest.

"The money is still here," shouted one of the men.

"Curse the money!" shouted the blind man. "Is Flint's packet still there?"

Obviously the blind man was not interested in the money in Bill's trunk. He wanted the packet of papers that I now held close to my beating heart.

After the men shouted down that the papers were nowhere to be seen, the blind man ordered them to find my mother and me. He knew that we must have taken what he wanted. But the men had had enough. They were satisfied with the gold coins and were unwilling to obey the harsh orders of the blind man.

Is Flint's Packet Still There?

Soon a quarrel began. The men all threatened each other and then the blind man.

This quarrel saved us. While it was still raging, another sound came from the top of the hill—the sound of approaching horses. The next sound I heard was a pistol shot, which was a warning of danger. As soon as they heard the shot, the men scattered in all directions. Only the blind man remained, tapping up and down the road in a frenzy and calling for his mates.

He took a wrong turn and began walking straight towards the approaching horses. He immediately realized his error and turned with a scream. He ran straight for a ditch, fell,and then got up again. But it was too late, for one horse was already upon him. He went down with a cry that rang high into the night. The four hooves trampled him to death.

I leaped to my feet and hailed the riders. They were men who had heard of our trouble

The Horse Was Upon the Blind Man.

and had decided to come to help us. They quickly revived my mother, but the blind man was stone dead.

We all went back to the inn, which had been ransacked and almost destroyed by the men who had searched it. I knew at once that the packet of papers I held must be very valuable. I asked the men if they would ride with me to Dr. Livesey's house right away. They seemed to understand my urgency and we set out at once.

The Inn Had Been Ransacked.

Jim Reaches Dr. Livesey's Door.

## Chapter 6
## The Captain's Papers

We rode as fast as we could until we finally reached Dr. Livesey's home. The house was dark, but I knocked several times at the door.

A servant answered and led me in to see the doctor. At once I told him what had happened. The doctor showed pride in my mother's great courage and praised me for my quick thinking. His friend, Squire Trelawney, also praised me. They asked the servant to bring me some warm food and drink.

After I had finished my meal, the doctor asked me if I still had the packet of papers.

I assured him that I did and handed him the oilcloth package.

"And now, squire," said the doctor to his friend, "you have heard of this man Flint, I suppose?"

"Heard of him!" cried the squire. "Heard of him, you say! He was the bloodthirstiest buccaneer that ever sailed. Blackbeard was a child compared to Flint!"

"Well, I've heard of him myself," said the doctor. "But the point is, did he have any money?"

"Money!" shouted the squire. "Why, what else would those villains be after but money?"

The doctor soon figured out that the packet contained some clue to Captain Flint's treasure. He asked me if I would allow him and the squire to open the packet. I of course agreed, since I was now even more eager than they were to see its contents.

Inside the packet was a ledger which re-

Those Villains Were After Money.

corded the exploits and the various amounts of money and jewels Captain Flint had collected in one way or another. But there was also a paper, which was sealed in several places with wax.

The doctor opened the seals with great care, and out fell the map of an island. It included all the particulars that would be needed to bring a ship safely to its shores. The island was about nine miles long and five miles across, and shaped like a fat dragon. It had a hill in the center marked the "Spyglass." There were three crosses made with red ink, under which were written: BULK OF TREASURE HERE. On the back of the map there were written directions on how to find the exact location of the treasure.

Dr. Livesey and the squire were filled with excitement.

"Livesey," said the squire, "you will give up your practice at once. Tomorrow I start for

A Map of an Island!

Bristol. In less than three weeks we will have the best ship and the best crew in all England. Hawkins will come as cabin boy. You will be the ship's doctor and I will be admiral. We'll take our loyal friends, Redruth, Joyce and Hunter. We'll set sail, find the treasure, and be rich for the rest of our lives!"

The doctor agreed at once, but he warned Squire Trelawney to keep all that he knew a deep secret. He knew that the men who had attacked the inn would not disappear, and if they got wind of our secret, we would pay with our lives. The squire nodded his head in agreement and went up to his room to prepare for his journey to Bristol.

We'll Be Rich for the Rest of Our Lives!

Jim Reads the Squire's Letter.

## Chapter 7
## I Go to Bristol

It took longer than we expected until we were finally ready to go to sea. During that time, I lived at the doctor's house and was under the charge of Redruth, the doctor's friend and gamekeeper. After several weeks, we finally received a letter from the squire.

His letter glowed with excitement. He had found a ship named the *Hispaniola*, which he claimed was most seaworthy. Then he explained that, quite by accident, he met an old sailor with one leg. The sailor had been a ship's cook and wanted to return to the sea.

He promised the squire that he could find him the best crew in England.

Trelawney was very taken with this man, whose name was Long John Silver. He assured us that the fellow was honest, hard working, and quite clever. He also owned a tavern in the town and had a decent-sized bank account.

The letter filled me with excitement and expectation. We were to leave for Bristol the very next day. I hurriedly ran to say goodbye to my mother, who was managing the inn quite well.

That night I could hardly sleep, I was so filled with dreams of exciting adventures at sea.

Dreams of Exciting Adventures at Sea

Jim Sees Ships of All Types and Sizes.

## Chapter 8
## At the Sign of the "Spy-Glass"

The ride to Bristol was long and uneventful. When I finally arrived, Squire Trelawney was there to meet me. We walked together along the docks, and to my great delight, I was able to see many ships of all sizes and types. In one, sailors were singing at their work: in another, seamen were climbing high above me on masts that seemed no thicker than a spider's web. Although I had lived by the shore all my life, it seemed I had never been near the sea till then.

When we finished eating our breakfast, the

squire gave me a note addressed to John Silver. He owned a tavern called the Spyglass, and I was to go there to meet him and give him the note.

I soon found the place. It was bright and freshly painted, the windows had neat red curtains, and the floor was cleanly sanded. As I was waiting, a man came out of a side room, and at a glance I was sure he must be Long John. His left leg was cut off close to the hip, and under the left shoulder he carried a crutch. He managed to get around quite well in spite of his handicap. He was very tall and strong, with a face as big as a ham. But there seemed something pleasant and intelligent about him. He whistled as he moved among the tables.

I had not forgotten what Captain Bill had told me long ago in the inn. He had been very wary of a one-legged seafaring man and had actually paid me to keep a lookout for the

Long John Silver

man. But one look at this man before me was enough. I had seen Black Dog and the blind man, whose name I found was Pew, and I was pretty sure I knew what a buccaneer was like. Long John didn't look like one.

So I got up my courage at once, crossed the threshold, and walked right up to the man and introduced myself. I was right, he was indeed Long John Silver. He took my hand in his large firm grasp.

Just then, one of the customers at the back of the tavern rose suddenly and made for the door. His haste attracted my attention, and I recognized him at once. It was Black Dog!

"Oh!" I cried. "Stop him! It's Black Dog!"

Long John sent one of his men out the door after the man. I explained that Black Dog was a buccaneer who had come to my own home not too long ago. Long John looked very serious and showed excitement and surprise.

"Well, I never—a buccaneer—here in my tavern. And with a name like Black Dog!"

Jim Recognizes Black Dog.

All the while he talked, Long John stumped up and down the tavern on his crutch, slapping tables with his hand. He gave such a show of outrage that it would have convinced even a judge. My suspicions had been awakened when I saw Black Dog at the tavern. But now Long John had me thoroughly convinced that he had never seen the man before.

He praised my sharp eyes for spotting the scoundrel and sat down to have a glass of rum. I immediately liked Long John. He seemed to have a sense of humor and an adventuresome spirit.

After this incident with Black Dog, Long John and I walked back to the ship. On the way he told me all about the different ships that we passed by—their rig, tonnage, and nationality. He related bits of stories and jokes he had heard at sea. I began to see that here was one of the best of possible shipmates.

Long John Tells Jim About Ships.

When we got to the ship, Dr. Livesey and the squire greeted us warmly. Long John told them what had happened from beginning to end with a great deal of spirit and total honesty.

"That was how it were, now, weren't it, Hawkins?" he would say now and again.

We all regretted that the scoundrel Black Dog had gotten away, but the squire soon cheered us all up with some good news. We would leave on our voyage the very next morning!

The Squire's Good News!

Captain Smollett Is Uneasy.

## Chapter 9
## The Captain and the Crew

After our meeting, the squire and the doctor introduced me to the ship's crew. The captain's name was Smollett, and the first mate was a weathered-looking old sailor named Arrow.

We had been in the squire's cabin only about five minutes when there was a knock at the door. It was Captain Smollett. He had come to tell the squire that he felt uneasy about the crew and our mission.

"I thought we were sailing on a secret mission," said Smollett, "and now I find that the crew is talking about going after treasure. Now, treasure is ticklish work. I don't like treasure voyages—especially when they are secret. But it seems that with this one, rumors are spreading like wildfire. Why, some of the men are even talking about a map with red crosses on it that show where the treasure is hidden."

The squire and the doctor exchanged looks of surprise and shock. They had told no one about the map. But somehow there had been a leak, and now the secret was not so well kept.

Dr. Livesey scratched his head and asked the captain what else he was worried about and what ideas he had for dealing with his misgivings about the voyage.

"Well," answered Smollett, "I don't like the looks of the crew—especially Arrow. He drinks a bit too much and he mixes too freely with the men. A mate should keep to himself.

The Secret Is Out!

What worries me about all of this is simply that I can't fully trust my own crew. And once we are out at sea, anything can happen.

"I only ask three things. First, I beg you to hide this map carefully and to keep it a secret—even from me. Second, the crew is just now loading the powder and the guns in the forehold. I suggest you have them put here under the cabin. Third, you are bringing four of your own people with you. Instead of putting them in the front of the ship, I advise you to keep them in the cabins here so they will be close by."

All the captain said made sense, but it had an air of foreboding about it. The doctor at once agreed to all of Smollett's suggestions, but the squire doubted his wisdom. He took an instant dislike to the captain and only agreed to go along with the doctor because he wanted to start the voyage peacefully.

The Captain Asks Three Things.

The whole crew sang.

# Chapter 10
## The Voyage

All that night we were in a great bustle, getting things stowed in their places and bidding farewell to all of the squire's friends.

It was a little before dawn when the boatswain sounded his pipe and the crew began to man the decks. As we pulled away from the dock, one of the men asked Long John—whom they all called Barbecue, since he was the cook—to sing a song. He at once broke out with the words I knew so well:

"Fifteen men on the Dead Man's Chest," And then the whole crew sang the chorus:

"Yo-ho-ho, and a bottle of rum!"

That exciting moment carried me back to the old Admiral Benbow Inn, and I could almost hear the voice of Captain Billy Bones piping in the chorus.

I am not going to relate the voyage in detail. It was fairly prosperous. The ship proved to be a good ship, the crew were capable seamen, and the captain knew his business well. But before we came to Treasure Island, two or three things happened that are important to my story.

Mr. Arrow turned out to be even worse than the captain had feared. He had no command among the men, and they ignored him when they wanted to. After a day or two at sea, he began to appear on deck with hazy eyes, red cheeks, and slurred speech. He was obviously drinking. But none of us could figure out where he got the rum. Of course, we had made it very plain that there would be

Arrow Had No Command Among the Men.

no rum or other alcohol allowed on board. No matter how carefully we watched him, we simply could not figure it out.

Arrow was not only useless as an officer and a bad influence among the men, but it was plain that at this rate he would soon kill himself. No one was very surprised nor very sorry when one night, during a rough sea, he disappeared entirely and was never seen again.

Long John, or Barbecue, as the crew called him, had great respect among the men. He was always kind to me and was always glad when I stopped by in the kitchen to talk with him.

"Come away, Hawkins," he would say, "come and have a yarn with John. Nobody's more welcome than yourself, my son. Here's Cap'n Flint—that's what I call my parrot, after the famous buccaneer—here's Cap'n Flint predicting success to our voyage."

Long John's Parrot—Captain Flint

And the parrot would say over and over, "Pieces of eight! Pieces of eight!" until I wondered why it was not out of breath.

We had some rough weather on the voyage, but as we neared our destination, we had a steady breeze and a quiet sea. The *Hispaniola* rolled steadily, dipping her bow now and then with a whiff of spray.

Just after sundown, when all my work was over and I was on my way to my berth, it occurred to me that I would like an apple. The squire had stocked the ship with several barrels of apples, which he thought would be pleasant for the crew.

When I looked into the large barrel, it seemed so dark that I couldn't tell if there were any apples left. So I got inside the barrel itself. Sitting there in the dark, with the sound of the water and the rocking movement of the ship, I either fell asleep or was on the point of doing so, when a heavy man sat down

A Look Inside the Apple Barrel

close by. The barrel shook as he leaned his shoulders against it. I was about to speak when I heard the man begin to talk. It was Long John Silver, and before I had heard a dozen words, I would not have shown myself for all the world. I lay there trembling and listening in fear and curiosity. I soon understood that the lives of all the honest men on board depended upon me alone.

Frightening Words!

Long John Reveals His Past.

## Chapter 11
## What I Heard in the Apple Barrel

"No, not I," said Silver. "Flint was cap'n. I was quartermaster because of my wooden leg. The same time I lost my leg, old Pew lost his eyes. That was some voyage, it was."

"Ah!" cried another voice. "Flint was the best there ever was!"

"We were the roughest crew afloat, we were. And we got ourselves plenty of gold on those voyages. That's how I was able to buy myself that little tavern and wait for the time to find the rest of Flint's treasure."

From what Silver was saying to his mate,

Israel Hands, I could figure out that he had known about our voyage from the start. Indeed, Silver had been a buccaneer with Captain Flint himself. Now, one by one, he was turning the crew into common pirates like him.

"What I want to know," asked Israel Hands, "is how long we intend to sit here quietly and wait. I've just about had it with Smollett. I want to break into their cabin. I want their fine food and wine. I want to let them know just who we *really* are."

"I'll give the word," answered Silver. "And it won't happen until the very last moment. Captain Smollett is a first-rate seaman, and we'll let him sail the ship for us. The squire and the doctor have the map, and I don't know where it is, do I? When the right time comes, after they've found the treasure for us, then we'll get rid of 'em. As my friend Billy Bones would say, 'Dead men don't bite.'"

Israel Hands Wants to Attack Now!

I was shivering with fear. I could hardly believe all that I had heard. Just then a sort of brightness fell upon me in the barrel. Looking up, I found the moon had risen and was shining on the foresail. I heard a voice shout, "Land ho!"

Land Is Sighted.

The Moon Was Shining.

## Chapter 12
## Council of War

As soon as everyone heard that land was spotted, there was a great rush of feet across the deck. When Long John and his mate were out of sight, I made my escape from the apple barrel.

Everyone had gathered on the top deck and was talking and gesturing with wild excitement. I felt as if I were in a dream. I was still in shock over what I had heard.

When Captain Smollett appeared on deck, he carried with him a map of the island. Long John's eyes burned in his head when he saw the paper, but I knew it wasn't what he expected. I could tell by the fresh look of the paper that this was not the same map we had found in Billy Bones' trunk. The map was an exact copy, except that it did not show the red crosses that marked the treasure sites. Even though he was disappointed, Silver was clever enough to hide it.

Long John acted so cool and collected that I could not help being amazed at his ability to hide his true feelings. I shuddered when he even looked my way.

As soon as I was able, I made my way over to the doctor. I told him that I had some important and frightening news. The doctor nodded and motioned towards his cabin. On the way there he alerted Captain Smollett and the squire. So by the time I reached his cabin the three men were waiting to hear me out.

As briefly as I could, I told my friends all

Long John Sees the Map.

I had overheard in the barrel. They remained silent for a few moments after I had finished. Then the doctor poured everyone a glass of red wine.

"Now, captain," the squire said to Smollett, "I see that you were right from the start. I was foolish not to have listened to you."

"Believe me," answered the captain, "I never saw a crew as sneaky as this one. They mean to mutiny but have cleverly disguised their true feelings all this time. That John Silver is a remarkable man!"

"He'd look more remarkable hanging from the gallows where he belongs!" added the doctor.

We then asked the captain for his advice. He acknowledged that we were in a bad position. We could not tell for sure how many of the men were loyal to us and how many were loyal to Silver. Since it was too late to turn back, we could only be wary and wait for the right moment to plan our next move.

The Captain Suspects a Mutiny.

The Island Looks Gray and Sad.

## Chapter 13
## My Shore Adventure Begins

The next morning I got my first look at the island. It was covered with gray-colored woods, and I could see yellow streaks of land between the trees. The hills ran up above the trees until they ended in naked rock jutting in sharp points towards the sky.

The island looked gray and sad. As the ship drew closer to shore, the birds flew over our heads and the waves thundered against the deck. I hated the very thought of setting foot on that island.

We had a dreary morning's work before us.

There was no sign of any wind. But the boats had to be manned and the ship had to be anchored. I volunteered to work on one of the small boats. The heat was sweltering, and the men grumbled fiercely over their work. As soon as land was sighted, the men began to show their real feelings. Mutiny was in the air. They no longer did their work cheerfully, and I could detect a feeling of open anger and resentment among them. I knew it would not be long before they turned against us. It was clear that Long John Silver was now calling the shots.

Captain Smollett detected what was happening and decided to give the men leave to go ashore. He figured that would give the squire, the doctor, and him time to plan their strategy.

I decided to go ashore with the men. So I slipped into one of the boats and sat quietly in the back. No one seemed to notice except

Jim Goes Ashore with the Men.

for Long John himself. He looked sharply over at me from another boat and called:

"Hawkins, is that you?"

From that time on, I began to regret what I had done.

The crew raced for the beach, but the boat I was in had the lead. As we went under some trees, I caught a branch and swung out, plunging myself into the nearest bush. I heard Long John shout my name, but I broke into a run and ran until I was out of sight of the boats.

Long John Spots Jim in the Boat.

A Snake Slithers Between the Foliage.

## Chapter 14
## Long John Strikes the First Blow

I was so pleased at having escaped that I began to enjoy myself and look around the strange island.

I had crossed a marshy tract full of willows and other swamp trees when I came upon a piece of sandy country about a mile long. I examined the little flowering plants and watched snakes slither between the foliage.

Soon I heard voices, so I hid under an oak and sat straining to hear what was being said.

I immediately recognized Long John's voice.

He was talking with one of the mates. This man obviously had not known about the plan, and as Long John described it, the mate answered him angrily.

"I thought you were an honest man," he said. "Mutiny is not my style. I'm an honest sailor and I curse the day I joined this crew."

Just then a cry of anger echoed over the hill. Then we all heard one long, horrible scream.

"What was that?" shouted the mate.

"That?" returned Silver with a sly smile. "That was the last sound of your friend Joseph—another honest sailor. He too wouldn't go along with my little plan."

"Joseph!" shouted the mate. "God rest his soul. And as for you, Long John, you're no mate of mine. If I die like a dog, I'll die doing what's right. Kill me too if you can, but I dare you!"

And with that, this brave fellow turned his

Jim Overhears Long John's Threat.

back directly on Long John and set off towards the beach. He did not get very far. With a cry, John grabbed the branch of a tree, whipped the crutch out of his armpit, and sent it hurtling through the air. It struck the poor fellow with incredible force right in the middle of his back. His hands flew up and he fell to the ground.

I couldn't tell how badly he was injured, but from his groans I would guess that his back was broken. He had no time to recover. Silver was on top of him in a moment and buried his knife in the fallen body. I could hear him pant loudly as he stabbed the mate.

I felt myself grow dizzy and I knew I was about to faint. I blacked out for only a second. The sound of the birds screaming overhead brought me to. I saw the monster, John Silver, put his hat upon his head as if nothing had happened. Then he simply cleaned his knife and put it away.

Joseph Fell to the Ground.

Stepping over the body of his poor victim, Long John gave three shrill whistles that rang in the air. He was calling his men. They already had killed two mates, and I couldn't help wondering if I was their next victim.

My heart pounding, I ran silently through the bushes. I had no idea where I was going. I only knew I had to get away. I was so frightened I could hear my own heartbeats and feel the sweat as it streamed down my neck.

I soon found myself among some pine trees. Here I saw a sight that brought me to a total standstill.

Jim Runs for His Life.

Is It a Man or a Beast?

# Chapter 15
# The Man of Treasure Island

There under the pine trees, I saw a figure leap swiftly behind a tree. I could not be sure if it was a man or a beast. It seemed dark and shaggy. All I knew was that no beast could be worse than Long John Silver.

I stood stock still and did not attempt to hide or run away. The shaggy creature came out from behind the tree and held out his hands toward me. I immediately saw that this shaggy, ragged creature was indeed a man.

"Who are you?" I asked.

"Ben Gunn," he answered in a hoarse and almost rusty-sounding voice. "I'm poor Ben Gunn, I am, and I haven't spoken with another human being for three years."

I could see now that he was an Englishman like me. His skin, where it was exposed, had been burned by the sun. He was dressed in the most incredible rags I had ever seen. They were mere tatters of an old ship's sail. On his waist he wore an old brass-buckled belt.

"Three years!" I cried. "Were you shipwrecked?"

"No, mate," he said, "I was marooned."

I had heard that word before. I knew it stood for a horrible punishment where pirates would actually put someone ashore on a desolate and distant island. They would not provide the unfortunate sailor with food or drink. Most men in this situation would not survive.

But old Ben Gunn was a clever man. He

Ben Gunn, the Marooned Sailor

told me how he had learned to live off the berries and fruits he had found on the island and the oysters and fish in its waters.

"Do you happen to have some cheese with you?" he asked. "Many's the long night I've dreamed of cheese—toasted and dripping off a thick slab of brown bread. Then I wake up and I'm still here on this lonely island."

I assured Ben Gunn that I had nothing at all with me, but if I ever got back on board the *Hispaniola*, he could have cheese by the pound.

After the old man asked me my name, he asked if I was sailing with Flint. I assured him that Flint was long since dead. Next he asked me if Long John Silver was on the ship. Seeing how afraid he was, I decided I'd better tell him the whole story.

He heard my tale with great interest, and when I was through he told me I was a good lad. He wanted to know whether he would be

Ben Describes His Dream of Cheese.

rewarded if he were to help me and my friends aboard the ship. He asked for a thousand dollars and passage home.

I assured him that the squire was a gentleman, and he would greatly reward any favor that would get us all out of this terrible trouble. Upon hearing this, Ben Gunn showed much relief and told me this story.

He was among Flint's crew when the captain buried the famous treasure. When Flint went on shore, he took six strong mates with him to bury the chest. After one week, Flint came back—alone. He had killed all six of the mates. No one knew how he did it, and only Flint knew where the treasure was buried. Billy Bones and Long John were aboard the ship. When they saw Flint come back alone, they asked him where the treasure was hidden. All he answered was, "Go ashore if you like. This ship sails tonight." So they sailed away and old Flint kept his secret.

Ben Tells of the Murderous Captain Flint.

Three years later, Ben Gunn was aboard another ship. He sighted this island and recognized it as the one where Flint had buried his treasure. He convinced his mates to go ashore and hunt for the gold. They searched for twelve days in the sweltering sun and found nothing. Each day they grew more angry at Ben. On the thirteenth day, they handed Ben a gun, a spade, and an axe, and told him he could stay on Treasure Island and hunt for Flint's money as long as he pleased.

Just as Gunn finished his story, I heard the thunder of a cannon.

"They have begun to fight!" I cried. "Follow me."

I began to run towards the shore while close at my side, Ben Gunn trotted easily and lightly. He talked constantly, but I could hardly hear or understand a word of it.

Soon I saw the British flag fluttering in the air above the trees. One look, and I knew that

Ben's Mates Marooned Him on the Island.

this must be where the doctor, the squire, and Captain Smollett had set up camp on the island. That flag meant safety for me.

Rushing Towards the British Flag

The Captain and Hunter Go Ashore.

## Chapter 16
## The Captain Tells How the Ship Was Abandoned

"It was about one-thirty when two boats left the *Hispaniola* to go ashore. The doctor, the squire,and I were talking matters over in the cabin. Hunter, one of the crew members, came to tell us that Jim Hawkins had slipped into a boat and gone ashore with the rest.

"We were worried about Jim and afraid we would never see the lad again. We decided that Hunter and I would go ashore in one of the lifeboats and see if we could find Jim.

139

"We sailed towards the small stockade that had been built on the island. I had a pistol hidden under my jacket and was ready for anything.

"We were already ashore when I heard a bloodcurdling scream. It was the scream of a man at the point of death. My first thought was that Jim Hawkins, poor lad, had been captured and killed by Silver and his crew.

"I knew we had little time to waste. So we returned immediately to the lifeboat. Hunter rowed powerfully, and we were soon back on board the ship.

"The squire and the doctor were white-faced with fear. Even Hunter was shaking with fright.

"We made a daring plan. Holding off the crew with our guns, we loaded the lifeboat with necessary supplies. We were going ashore to fight it out with Silver and his crew. There was nothing else we could do.

Loading the Lifeboat with Supplies

"We made it to shore safely with the first load, then we decided to risk a second try. We knew we would need guns, ammunition and food if we were to stay alive.

"By this time the tide was beginning to ebb, and the ship was swinging round to its anchor. Redruth—the doctor's companion, the squire, the doctor, Hunter, and two crew men—Joyce and Gray—joined me as we shoved off in the lifeboat, which was heavy with supplies."

A Second Trip Ashore

A Perfect Target in the Sea

## Chapter 17
## The Doctor Tells of the Lifeboat's Last Trip

"The last trip to the island was the most difficult. The boat was loaded down with goods and supplies, and this time all seven of us were aboard. The sea was beginning to get rough, and it took all our skill to keep from being swept off course.

"When we were about midway between the ship and the island, I saw, to my horror, that Long John's men aboard the *Hispaniola* were loading the cannon and aiming it at our little boat. And the worst of it was that we were right out in the middle of the sea—a perfect target.

"I could hear as well as see that rascal, Israel Hands, plumping down a round of fire on the deck.

" 'Who's the best shot?' asked the captain.

" 'Mr. Trelawney is,' I answered.

" 'Mr. Trelawney, will you please pick off one of those men, sir? Israel Hands, if possible,' said the captain.

" The squire was as cool as steel. He aimed his gun and fired. There was a great commotion on board, but the shot passed right over the head of Israel Hands and downed one of the other mates. It was clear that they did not intend to let this stop them. They never so much as looked at their fallen mate though he was not dead, and I could see him trying to crawl away.

"We pulled on the oars with great effort while fire passed over our heads. One of the

The Fire Passed Over Our Heads.

shots must have hit us in the stern, since the boat began to sink. Luckily, by this time we were close to shore, and the captain and I found ourselves standing in three feet of water. There were no lives lost and we all reached shore safely. But our supplies were gone. To make things worse, only two guns out of five remained in a state of service.

"To add to our worries, we could hear Silver's men on shore, and we knew we'd have to make a run for it if we were to reach the stockade alive."

No Lives Were Lost.

I Approached the Stockade.

## Chapter 18
## Jim Continues the Story

I approached the stockade with great care. I knew the doctor and his crew had reached the island safely, since they had already strung up the flag. But there was a great deal of fighting going on. Silver's men were shooting at the cabin, and the doctor and his crew were fighting back with all they had.

I bid farewell to Ben Gunn, who reminded me of my promise. He told me where he could be found and asked that whoever looked for him should carry a white banner, so he'd know there was no danger.

I hid for some time watching the attack. Silver's men were demolishing the lifeboat with their axes. Boats kept coming and going between the ship and the island. The men shouted and laughed, and I could tell they had been drinking rum.

Finally I made my way to the cabin. The doctor couldn't believe his eyes when he saw me. He had taken me for dead. I told him and the men my story. Next, I looked carefully around the cabin. It was a log house made of unsquared trunks of pine. There was a porch at the door and under the porch was a little spring of fresh water. There was not much inside the house, just a stone slab to sit on and an old rusty iron basket in which to make a fire.

If we had been allowed to sit idle, we would have become bored and unhappy, but Captain Smollett was too smart to let that happen. He called us all together and divided us into

Destroying the Lifeboat

watches: the doctor, Gray, and I for one; the squire, Hunter, and Joyce for the other. Tired though we all were, two were sent for firewood and two were to bring water from the spring. I was put on as sentry at the door, and the captain moved among all of us, keeping our spirits up and lending a hand.

From time to time the doctor came to the door for a little air, and whenever he did he talked with me.

"That man Smollett," he said, "is a better man than I am. And when I say that, it means a lot."

Another time he asked me more about Ben Gunn. I told him that I could not be entirely sure that the old man was sane. The doctor explained that no man who had been left all alone for three years could be expected to appear normal, but the fact that he had managed to survive indicated a certain amount of sanity. He told me that he had with him

Gathering Firewood and Water

a small amount of cheese that he was saving for Ben Gunn. He had a feeling we would be needing the old man's services sooner than we thought.

That evening, we speculated upon our chances for survival. The doctor figured that the rum and the climate would be working against our enemies. Those that didn't get too drunk to fight would get ill from sleeping outside beside the marsh. The captain hoped that eventually they would give up and return to the ship and get to buccaneering again.

I was dead tired, and as soon as the sun went down I got to sleep. I was awakened by the early sun and the sound of someone shouting:

"Flag of truce!"

Awakened by the Sun and by Shouting

Is the White Cloth a Trap?

## Chapter 19
## Silver's Proposal

Sure enough, there were two men just outside the stockade, and one of them was waving a white cloth. That man was Long John Silver himself.

The captain urged us all to stay inside and to keep our guns ready. He didn't trust Long John, and he suspected a trap of some sort. Then he turned to the two men and shouted to them in a loud voice to state their demands. Silver answered that he wished to meet with the captain to make terms.

The captain made it very clear that if there

was any treachery on Silver's part, he would pay with his life. Then he gave Long John a signal, and the one-legged mate slowly worked his way up the hill to the stockade. He had a terrible time getting up the steep incline, as his crutch slipped several times in the soft sand. But he stuck to it. At last he arrived before the captain and saluted in a formal manner.

The two men sat down on the porch and filled their pipes.

"Now here it is," said Silver. "We know you have the map and we aim to get it. If you give us the chart, we can stop all this fighting and killing. Once we've found the treasure, you can come aboard with us, and I give you my word you will be put ashore safely. Or you can stay here, and I promise I will send the first ship we meet to rescue you and your mates."

Captain Smollett rose from his seat and

Silver Makes an Offer to the Captain.

faced Long John. He made it very clear that if Long John and his men were willing to surrender to him, he would take the whole crew back to England for trial. Those were his only terms. He knew that the pirates could not find the treasure without the map, and he knew that none of them were expert enough to sail the ship safely back to England.

Long John grew angry, his eyes burned with wrath, and he put out his pipe.

"Give me a hand up!" he cried.

"Not I," answered the captain.

Not one of us moved to help Silver get back on his crutch. Growling and cursing, he crawled along the sand until he got hold of the porch and hoisted himself up on his crutch.

He spat on the ground and stumbled off to return to his crew.

Silver Stumbles Off.

Silver's Crew Leap from the Woods.

# Chapter 20
# The Attack

As soon as Silver was out of sight, the captain ordered us to return to our posts. He knew we had to prepare for an attack from Silver's crew. There was no time to lose. He urged us to eat a hearty breakfast, as we soon would be needing all our strength. Then we loaded our guns and began the wait.

After a long time, we heard the sound of gunfire. A bunch of Silver's crew leaped from the woods and ran straight for our stockade. At the same moment, fire opened from the woods, and a rifle shot sang through the doorway, knocking the doctor's gun to bits.

The invaders swarmed over the fence like monkeys. The squire and the doctor fired again and again. Three men fell, but one wasn't hit. He got on his feet and retreated into the woods.

Four men were now within our territory. They ran straight towards us, shouting as they advanced. There was crossfire, but no one was downed. In a moment, the four pirates were upon us.

One pirate grabbed Hunter's gun by the muzzle, wrenched it from his hands, and threw it through the window. Then with one blow, he laid Hunter out cold. Meanwhile, another entered by a rear door and pulled his knife on the doctor.

The stockade was full of smoke, to which we owed our comparative safety, since it added to the confusion and blinded our enemy.

One Man Retreated Into the Woods.

The captain shouted to us to fight out in the open. I snatched my sword from a pile, and at that moment someone gave me a cut across my knuckles. I dashed out into the sunlight. Someone was close behind me. I reversed my position and tried to run around the other side of the cabin. In a flash, I found myself face to face with one of the pirates. He roared as he lifted his sword above his head. As he did this, I jumped to one side, missed my footing, and rolled headlong down the hill. When I was back on my feet, I saw from the bottom of the hill that the fight was ending. The pirates were in retreat and the victory was ours!

I made my way carefully back up the hill. The house was somewhat cleared of smoke, and I saw at a glance the price we had paid for our victory. Hunter was still out cold, and Joyce had been shot through the head.

Jim Dashed Out Into the Sunlight.

Treating the Wounded Captain

## Chapter 21
## My Sea Adventure Begins

There was no return of the mutineers—not so much as another shot out of the woods. They had accepted their defeat. As for us, we had a quiet time and saw to our own wounds. The captain had been badly wounded. Although no organ had been injured, his shoulder blade was broken, and this affected his lung. The doctor said he would be all right as long as he did not walk or move his arm for a few weeks. As for Hunter, do what we could, he never recovered consciousness.

My own accidental cut across the knuckles

was nothing, and the doctor patched it up in a few minutes. When he finished, the doctor informed me that he was going to see if he could find Ben Gunn. He had an idea that the old man could help us somehow.

In the meantime, the house was stifling hot and the little patch of sand outside was ablaze with the afternoon sun. I began to envy the doctor walking in the cool woods, with the birds and the smell of pine, while I sat grilling with my clothes stuck to me and the smell of death and dying all around.

It was at this time that I got it into my head to find Ben Gunn's homemade boat and return to the *Hispaniola* and cut her loose. I had the plan all figured out and I thought for sure it would work.

When no one was really looking, I made a run for it and escaped into the woods, leaving only two men to guard the stockade.

I trudged through the woods until I found

Jim Leaves to Carry Out His Plan.

my way to the shore. The cool air brushed against my face, and for a moment I almost imagined I was back home and this was all a horrible nightmare.

From the shore I could see the *Hispaniola* and could even hear the murmur of voices as the pirates walked along her decks. As night came, the pirates boarded a lifeboat and made for the shore. I knew this was my chance, but I still had to find old Ben Gunn's little boat.

It was almost dark when I finally spied the craft beached beside a large rock. It was tiny, but it had been well made and I knew it would serve my purpose. Before setting out, I ate the food I had taken with me before I left the stockade. The last rays of daylight dwindled and disappeared, and absolute blackness settled down on Treasure Island.

Jim Finds Ben Gunn's Boat.

Jim Rows Towards the Ship.

## Chapter 22
## Israel Hands

When at last I was sure that I could row out to sea without being spotted, I untied the tiny boat and rowed quietly towards the *Hispaniola*. The sea was calm, and this helped me manage the tiny boat and bring it into position beside the ship. When I was only a few yards from the *Hispaniola*, I could see the yellow lantern light shining out from the lower porthole. The ship seemed to be empty except for one member of Silver's crew—Israel Hands. This was the very same man I had overheard plotting with Long John while I was hiding in the apple barrel. He was obviously wounded, and as I hoisted myself up to the porthole, I could see a dead man lying on the cabin floor. There had been a fight. Israel Hands had been the victor, but he was now badly wounded and alone. I knew this was a perfect opportunity to carry out my plan.

I managed to climb aboard the ship and silently pull out my knife and cut the rope which anchored the vessel. Once aboard, I lost no time in deciding to confront Hands in person.

When he saw me, Israel Hands nearly jumped out of his skin in surprise. But due to his condition, he could do little more than groan in pain. His leg had a great open bleeding stab wound and he could barely move. I soon informed him that I was now captain of this ship and I had come to take over. His only reply was a nod and a request for some

A Dead Man Is on the Cabin Floor.

brandy and food. I went below and brought up some supplies, then prepared a dinner for the two of us. I also bandaged his wound and helped him get on his feet. After some food and drink, Israel Hands sat up straighter, spoke clearer, and seemed well on his way to recovery.

I formed a pact with the wounded seaman. I agreed to dress his wounds if he would help me steer the ship to a secluded part of the island. In this way, Silver and his men would lose their only means of escape, and I would be able to help my friends flee the island in safety.

The wind was in our favor, and just as the sun began to rise on a new day, I had the *Hispaniola* safely on her course towards the far side of Treasure Island. When it was clear that the ship was in hand, Israel asked me to go down below and fetch him some wine. He claimed that the brandy had suddenly

Jim Bandages Israel Hands' Wounds.

become too strong for his taste. It was obvious that he wanted me to leave the deck. I knew he was up to something, but I agreed to go below. As soon as I was out of his sight, I removed my shoes and peered out from the lower deck.

He had risen from his position, and although he was still in great pain, it was clear that he once again had full use of his legs. In a minute he reached the supply box, pulled a long knife out from under some rope, and concealed it in his jacket. Now I knew that I must move fast or I would join the other mate whose body lay on the cabin floor.

Just at that time, the *Hispaniola* struck land, and both of us found ourselves rolling off the deck into the water. I was on my feet in seconds and waded slowly to shore. Hands was not far behind me, and despite his bad leg he moved quickly. When he was within range of my pistol, I stopped, waved the weapon in the air, and shouted:

The Hispaniola Struck Land.

"One more step, Mr. Hands, and I'll blow your brains out!"

He stopped instantly, and I could see that he was trying to think. At last he spoke and conceded that I had out-tricked him, and he was willing to give in.

I was drinking in his words and smiling away at my own cleverness when something flew through the air. In that instant Hands had thrown his knife, and I found my shoulder ripped open and bleeding. Without hesitation, I fired my pistol and a second later I heard a choked cry. Israel Hands plunged headfirst into the sea, never to breathe again.

Don't Take Another Step!

Eager to See His Friends Again

## Chapter 23
## In the Enemy's Camp

I began to feel sick and faint. The hot blood from my wound was running over my back and chest. I made my way back to the ship, went below, and cleaned and dressed my wound. Then I made sure the ship was securely anchored on the beach. This done, I began to make my way back to my companions with the good news.

After a long walk, I finally came to the clearing that marked the stockade. I could see a fire burning, and my heart lightened when I realized that I would soon be with my friends again.

I made my way slowly to the door of the cabin. It seemed that everyone was fast asleep, and I blamed myself for leaving them so shorthanded that there was no one to stand watch.

I walked carefully inside the cabin and stepped silently over the sleeping bodies. Just then I heard a shrill voice break forth in the darkness.

"Pieces of eight! Pieces of eight!"

It was Silver's parrot. I had no time to move, for in a flash Silver himself was upon me, and I realized that I had been captured.

The buccaneers lit torches and gathered around me. Silver laughed as he saw the look of fear upon my face. He explained that early that morning the doctor had come to inform him that the *Hispaniola* had been set adrift. Neither of the two men knew where she was or what had happened. The doctor gave Long John the cabin, and he and his companions moved their headquarters to another part of

Captured by Long John Silver

the island.

When he told me all this, I asked Long John if the doctor had asked after me. Silver nodded and said that Dr. Livesey was pretty angry that I had deserted them when the captain was ill and they needed all the men they had.

By this time the rest of the crew were demanding that Silver shoot me on the spot, but the old pirate would hear none of it. He still had a trick or two up his sleeve and said that I would come in useful as a hostage if and when the ship was found. Soon the men got hot-tempered and began to threaten Silver himself. They claimed that he was playing both sides and he could no longer be trusted.

In a dramatic moment, Long John reached inside his pocket and threw a paper on the cabin floor. It was Captain Flint's map of the treasure!

Silver Throws the Map on the Cabin Floor.

The Doctor Comes to Tend the Sick Pirates.

## Chapter 24
## The Plan

When the men saw the map, all talk of opposing Long John ceased. They were so anxious they could hardly sleep. As for me, I was still confused as to how or why the doctor had given up the stockade and the treasure map.

Early the next morning, my questions were answered, as the doctor himself came to visit us. He brought with him medicine and bandages to tend to the sick pirates. When he saw me, he only frowned and went on with his business. When he was through, he asked

Long John if he might have a word with me. The old pirate readily agreed.

The doctor put his hand on my shoulder and asked where I'd been. When I told him about my adventure, his face lit up. He explained that this was good news. Now that he knew the ship was safe, we all had a good chance for escape. He said no more, only that I should trust him.

Just then, Long John came back and informed the doctor that he was going to begin the hunt for the treasure that very morning. The doctor smiled and warned him to be careful and to keep me at his side. Then he shook my hand, winked, and walked off into the woods.

Something was up, but I knew better than to doubt the doctor. If there was a plan—and I knew that there was—it would be best to go along with it and say nothing.

The Doctor Has a Plan.

A Hearty Breakfast

## Chapter 25
## The Treasure Hunt

After all the pirates had been tended to by the doctor, we gathered around the fire for a hearty breakfast. Long John assured his crew that after we found the treasure and were off to sea, I would join them. In the meantime, having me along on the hunt would be insurance against any tricks the doctor might have planned.

The men then armed themselves with axes and shovels, and we all set off in the direction of the hill called the "Spy-glass."

We followed the directions on the map to

the letter. When we had gone over two miles, one of the men began to cry aloud, as if in terror. We heeded his shouts and ran towards him. When we reached the spot upon which he was standing we saw the reason for his cries. At the foot of a pine tree lay a human skeleton. A chill struck my heart. It must have been one of the men Flint had taken ashore when he first buried the treasure.

Long John examined the bones. They had been bleached white by the sun, but they seemed to lie in a peculiar position. Indeed, the body lay perfectly straight—his feet pointing in one direction, his hand raised above his head like a diver's, pointing directly the opposite way.

Silver took out his compass. The skeleton was pointing directly east. Flint had left a dead man's bones to point the way to the treasure.

Soon the men began to talk of death and

A Human Skeleton!

ghosts and the spirit of Captain Flint himself. They were frightened, and as we moved among the swaying trees we heard a faint cry:

"Darby M'Graw," it wailed, "Darby M'Graw, fetch me the rum!"

The men froze in their tracks. Those had been Captain Flint's last words. The men would have run away, but fear kept them together.

"Listen," said Silver, "that was an echo. It was like Flint's voice, but not exactly. It sounded more like someone else to me." He scratched his head for a minute and then said:

"Ben Gunn! That's who it sounds like. Why, alive or dead, old Ben Gunn was no one to fear, now was he, mates?"

The men at once picked up, and the color returned to their faces. They were not likely to let any man, alive or dead, get in their way now that they were so close to treasure.

The Men Freeze in Their Tracks.

Soon we approached the site of the treasure. The men nearly ran over me in their excitement.

We were now at the edge of the woods.

"Here, here, mates, all together!" shouted one of the crew.

And suddenly, not more than ten yards away I saw them all come to a dead stop. Before them stood a great gaping hole.

All was now clear. Someone had found the treasure and taken it—Silver had been tricked at his own game!

A Great Gaping Hole!

Stand By for Trouble.

# Chapter 26
# Silver's Men Rebel

The men stood stock still as they stared into the dark and empty excavation. Silver handed me a pistol and whispered, "Take that and stand by for trouble."

At the same time, he quietly began to move away from the crew. I was so revolted by his change of loyalty that I could not help whispering, "So, you've changed sides again."

Before he had time to answer, the pirates began swearing and shaking their fists.

One of the men called the others around, and facing Long John, he said in a loud, clear voice:

"Mates, there's the two of them alone there. One's the old cripple who brought us here, and the other's that boy—and I mean to get the both of 'em."

He was raising his arm and his voice, and he plainly meant to lead an attack. But just then—crack! crack! crack! Three shots flashed out of the thicket. Three pirates fell where they stood, and the other three ran for it with all their might.

At that moment, the doctor, Gray, and Ben Gunn joined us. They held pistols which were still smoking from the gunfire.

"Thank you kindly, doctor," said Long John as he mopped his face. "You came in the nick of time. And so it *is* you, Ben Gunn!" he added. "I never thought I'd see the likes of you again!"

The doctor sat down on a rock and explained what really had happened from the start.

The Pirates Are Attacked.

Ben, in his long and lonely wanderings around the island, had somehow found Flint's treasure. He had dug it up and in many weary journeys had carried it on his back to a hiding place in a cave on the other side of the island.

The doctor had wormed this secret from him on the afternoon of the attack. The next morning, when he saw the ship was gone, the doctor paid Long John a visit. He gave him the map, which was now useless, and possession of the stockade. The purpose of this was to get a chance to move safely from the stockade to the cave where Gunn had hidden the treasure. Being closer to the cave meant the doctor and his men would be farther away from the possibility of infection from malaria and nearer to the treasure, which had to be guarded. But when the doctor learned that I was being held by Silver and his men, he had to change some of his plans. He knew that when the crew discovered that the treas-

The Doctor Gives Long John the Map.

ure had been removed, there would be a revolt and that Long John probably would be executed. But he now feared that I would be shot as well.

To head off the crew and ambush them, the doctor had to think of a way to slow the men down, so that he and Gray could hide in the bushes and ambush them at the treasure site. It was then that Ben Gunn got the idea to work on the superstitions of his former shipmates and to pretend that he was the ghost of Captain Flint. This gave the doctor and Gray time to set up their ambush of Silver's crew.

"Ah," said Silver when he had heard the story, "it was lucky for me that I had Hawkins here. You would have let old John be cut to bits and never even given it a thought."

"Not a thought," answered Dr. Livesey cheerily.

The next thing we did was prepare to find

Silver Is Thankful That Jim Was with Him.

Ben Gunn's cave and begin the task of moving the treasure aboard the *Hispaniola*. We all loaded into a small boat and rowed clear across the island.

Soon old Ben Gunn gave a shout, and we knew he had sighted the cave. We brought the craft ashore and entered the hiding place.

It was a large, airy cave with a little spring and a pool of clear water. The floor was sand. Before a big fire lay Captain Smollett. In a far corner I could see heaps of coins and piles of gold bars. This was the treasure we had come so far to seek and that had already cost the lives of seventeen men from the *Hispaniola*.

Captain Smollett smiled when he saw me. All was forgiven, and he shook my hand like an old friend.

That night we prepared a feast to celebrate our good fortune. We ate some of Ben Gunn's salted goat's meat and drank a bottle of wine

The Treasure Is in the Cave.

from the *Hispaniola*. Never were people more happy than we were that night. And there was Silver, eating along with the rest of us and smiling like an ordinary sailor—almost as if nothing at all had happened between us.

A Celebration!

Loading the Treasure

## Chapter 27
## The End of My Adventure

The next morning we got right to work, for transporting the treasure from the cave to the ship was a big job. We were well aware that three of Silver's men still remained on the island, so we posted one sentry to keep a lookout for them. Ben Gunn and Gray loaded sacks of gold and carried them one at a time to the ship, while I was kept busy packing the money into smaller bags.

It was a strange collection, for there were coins and paper money from all over the world. They came in all different shapes and sizes. There were strange-looking Oriental pieces, stamped with what looked like wisps of string or bits of spider's web, and round pieces that had holes bored through the middle. I was filled with wonder at all the different places Flint must have gone to collect this great treasure.

Day after day this work went on. Every evening a fortune had been stowed aboard, and every morning there was still more to be transported to the ship.

At last, after nearly four days, the doctor and I went strolling on the shoulder of the hill, and we heard the sound of voices.

"Heaven forgive them," said the doctor, "'tis the mutineers!"

"All drunk, sir," said the voice of Long John Silver.

We had allowed Silver complete freedom, although we were far from friendly to him. But nothing seemed to bother the old pirate,

Money from All Over the World!

and he went about the tasks assigned him with cheerful eagerness.

When the doctor suggested that some of the mutineers might be in need of medical treatment, Long John spoke up for the first time.

"I ask your pardon, sir," he said, "but you would be wrong to tend to those men. They would kill you in a minute, I am sure of it. I'm on your side now, and I'd hate to see our chances of a safe return ruined."

As much as he hated to admit it, the doctor knew that Long John was right and that we had no choice but to leave the three men on the island to shift for themselves. We left them all our supplies and some medicine and hoped that they would survive somehow.

By this time we had stowed all the treasure and were ready to set sail for home. Early the next morning we boarded the *Hispaniola* and bid farewell to Treasure Island.

As we sailed away, the three mutineers

Supplies and Medicine for the Mutineers

called to us and begged us to take them aboard, but we knew that we could not risk another plot to mutiny. The doctor hailed them and told them where they could find the supplies and the medicine.

At last, when they saw we were not turning back, they began to shoot at the ship. Their shots just missed Silver, and we stayed under cover until we were safely out of range.

We were so short of men that everyone on board had to do the work of two. The captain, who was still recovering from his wounds, lay on a mattress and gave orders.

It was just sundown when we laid anchor in our first port on the way home. It was a beautiful landlocked gulf, and we were immediately surrounded by shore boats full of natives selling luscious fruits and vegetables. The sights and smells of this wonderful place helped us to forget our dark and bloody experiences on Treasure Island.

We Sailed Away.

The doctor and the squire took me along, and we went ashore to pass the evening. When we returned to the *Hispaniola*, Ben Gunn was on deck alone, and he at once began to confess to us that Silver was gone. He had escaped in a shore boat a few hours after we left. Silver had not left empty-handed. He had taken a few sacks of coins and gold with him.

I think we were all pleased to be rid of him at last, for none of us were really sure what plans or tricks he still might have up his sleeve.

The voyage home was calm and uneventful. We got a few extra men to help us on board and made a good cruise back. Of the original crew, there were now only five men left. But we were not as bad as the other ship which sailors sang about:

"With one man of her crew alive,
What put to sea with seventy-five."

Silver Has Escaped!

All of us got a fair share of Flint's treasure, and we all used it as we pleased. Captain Smollett used his share to buy a little house in the country and retire from his life at sea. This last voyage had showed him that the quiet life was more to his liking. Gray saved his money and put a good part of it towards studying the more technical aspects of his profession. Now he is a mate and part owner of a fine full-rigged ship. He also married his childhood sweetheart and started a family.

As for Ben Gunn, he got a great deal of Flint's treasure, since he was the one who led us to it to begin with. Unfortunately, those three years alone on Treasure Island did more damage to his mind than any of us had suspected. He went so wild with the comforts of civilization that he gambled and drank away all of his money in nineteen days. On the twentieth day he was begging in the streets. Then some seafaring men took pity

Ben Gunn Spent His Money Quickly.

on him and gave him an inn to take care of. He still lives there and is a great favorite of the men, as well as being a notable singer in church every Sunday.

The doctor returned to his practice and opened a free clinic for the poor. He is well-known for his medical skills and his generosity to the needy.

None of us ever heard of Long John Silver again. I believe that he has gone out of all our lives forever. I do know that he never returned to his wife and family who were waiting for him in Bristol. Perhaps they all met somewhere and are living a life of peace and luxury on some remote island. I hoped so, for his chances for comfort in another world are very small.

The three mutineers that were left on the island were never seen in England again. But who knows, they might have been saved by some other vessel and are continuing their life at sea.

A Notable Church Singer

As for me, I am content to spend the rest of my days safely on the land. I will never forget the excitement of those days at sea, but nothing could drag me back to the sea or to Treasure Island.

When I returned to England with my treasure, I went to visit my mother. She was overjoyed to see me. She had been managing the inn, and for the first time in many years, she was happy and making a good living. I wanted to share my good fortune with her, but she would have none of it.

For many months I pondered how to spend the rest of my life. I visited the doctor often and spent many hours talking these things over with him.

My mother took ill, and although I gave her the best care money could buy, she died in the spring. The inn was left in my care. Both my father and mother had spent all their lives taking care of sailors and travel-

Back Home at the Inn

ers. It was now my turn to carry on the family tradition.

One afternoon a gentleman from London came by the inn. He was impressed with the place and offered to buy it from me. He was tired of the city life and looked forward to spending his old age by the sea.

After visiting the doctor to talk things over, I decided to sell the inn.

In less than a month the deal was sealed. I shook hands with the elderly gentleman who was to take over what had been my home for so long.

I still live by the sea, and although I no longer take care of sailors, I have never lost interest in ships and tales of high adventure. But sometimes, when I hear the surf beating against the coast, I sit upright as if woken from a bad dream. For I can hear the sharp voice of Captain Flint still ringing in my ears: "Pieces of eight! Pieces of eight!"

A New Owner for the Inn?

Hearing Old Voices from the Sea

Admiral Benbow Inn

"Pieces of Eight! Pieces of Eight!"